Love it, love it, love it!

I have been out in this crazy dating market for the last several years. You have no idea the madness I've experienced.

People date, but do not ask the right questions when looking for a partner.

They get caught up in the emotional aspects and forget about the practical aspects as well as how they or a potential partner were raised.

I've noticed that people do not know what to ask either until things come up. You can't predict everything, but a lot can be covered in advance.

Don't wait to ask the right questions until it is too late because you're already deeply involved in the wrong relationship.

S. Johannes

Knowing Your Life Partner:

25 Questions to Ask and Answer

Free Audio Version Included

Amy Rose Herrick

Profit-Building Specialist

International Best-Selling Author

Published by Amy Rose Herrick

Herrick, Amy Rose

Knowing Your Life Partner: 25 Questions to Ask and Answer

First edition

Christiansted, US Virgin Islands: Amy Rose Herrick, 2024

 xvi, 88 pages, 9 inches

Relationships | Marriage | Finances | Compatibility | Insurance | Estate Planning | Medical | Household | Religious

978-1-960427-01-4

2023939487

306.764

 Amy Rose Herrick's books may be purchased in bulk for premiums, groups, educational, business or sales promotional use. For information, please write to: Amy@AmyRoseHerrick.com.

Disclaimer: The information and/or documents contained in this book do not constitute legal or financial advice and should never be used without first consulting with other professionals to determine what may be best for your individual needs. The publisher and the author do not make any guarantee or other promise as to any results that may be obtained from using the content of this book. The publisher and the author make no guarantees concerning the level of success you may experience by following the advice and strategies contained in this book, and you accept the risk that results will differ for everyone. Although the publisher and the author have made every effort to ensure that the information in this book was correct at press time, and while this publication is designed to provide accurate information in regard to the subject matter covered, the publisher and the author assume no responsibility for errors, inaccuracies, omissions, or any other inconsistencies herein and hereby disclaim any liability to any party for any loss, damage, or disruption caused by errors or omissions, whether such errors or omissions result from negligence, accident, or any other cause. If any names are used in any illustration, they have been changed to protect the privacy of the individual

DEDICATION

To My Past and Present Clients,

Thank you for sharing so many real-life experiences with me over the decades while we worked through all the financial issues.

We enjoyed the easy, joyful, celebration times and we journeyed together through the expected and unexpected difficult times too.

It is a privilege and an honor for me to be entrusted with helping you to navigate the financial parts of your lives.

May your relationship that you are building today be one filled with joy, happiness, great memories and be long lasting.

CONTENTS

CHAPTER	PG #

To access your free audio version, please use this link:

https://www.moneywithamyaudiobooks.com/25-questions-for-couples

INTRODUCTION

In case you are wondering, no, I am not an expert on relationships. What I can share with you and the reason for penning this title is a very strong conviction, from experience, that your relationship with a partner will be the foundational building blocks for everything else in your life. Your long-term relationship with a romantic partner definitely comes into play on all the financial work I do with couples and entrepreneurs.

I will share I am in my second marriage. We have been working at this union for over 40 years so far and are still learning how to navigate new chapters of change every year.

Dating, courtship, hooking up, finding a mate or whatever you choose to call the selection process for a life mate is not the same day-to-day relationship that a long-term romantic relationship may evolve into over a lifetime.

Unfortunately, for most of us, good looks, slim figures, great hair, perfect teeth, our best manners, endless energy, and even taunt muscles only last so long.

Wealth and health can change suddenly, for the better or for the worst.

No matter how much you seek after it or how powerfully it pulls your heartstrings, love is often not powerful enough to conquer every emotional or relationship-related issue.

Some relationships fail to be long-term with or without marriage certificates.

Hopeful promises were made, and future dreams were shared before they ended with some promises that could not be kept or dreams that could be fully realized.

By reading this book and being willing to ask, answer, and discuss the hard questions before you are deeply committed to a potential relationship, you are showing that you are looking for tools to be successful in what, for some, has been an elusive desire: a long-term loving relationship.

It takes courage to complete these exercises. It takes courage to tell the truth about how you really feel about an issue when you do not know how the other person feels about your answers.

It takes courage to listen to every word spoken, to understand how another person you are thinking about spending your life with feels about the same topic, especially when you disagree.

These short, thought-provoking questions were created to help you as a couple to talk through the issues that, if left unchecked, could destroy your relationship over time.

Each question has space for each of you to write your thoughts if you choose to. Some questions may sound silly to you in the context of your life experience.

Some may make you laugh.

Some answers given by your partner could upset you.

Other answers could result in the assurance you are both in total agreement on the topic. Ask!

Listening is the key.

Do not get distracted formulating your response while the other person is still talking. You cannot listen and formulate a response at the same time.

Be realistic.

If your partner is 100% passionate about an issue and you are barely 5%, can you be supportive and do it their way with ease?

Will your chosen one give you the support you need to proceed on an issue your way when you are 80% passionate about choice "A" and they are 50% to go either way when choices "A" & "B" are very different?

Will you meet somewhere in the middle that is agreeable to both of you? Do you intend to really do your best trying to compromise as conflicts arise? Do you already compromise easily?

Is even thinking about working out a compromise in a discussion difficult for you?

Is it your rule to never compromise?

Do not try to do all 25 questions in the same marathon session. Take the time needed to listen and be heard.

Here are some quick, simple ideas on how to approach the twenty-five probing questions in the following chapters:

One question a day will take a little less than a month to cover all 25 questions.

Make slips of paper numbered from 1 to 25. Put them in a jar or bowl. You will each pull one slip at a time out of a jar at random per session. The final session is three questions. This will take you 12 sessions to complete.

Doing one chapter at a time will take you nine sessions.

There is no question included here in this book that is off-limits for discussion. Every question should be answered by both individuals. No skipping the hard ones to only do the easy ones!

I grouped the questions in sections allowing you to choose where to start if my suggested format is not your priority. These sections are not necessarily in order of importance. They are compiled in this order only to help you move easily through a variety of broad relationship areas.

There is no magic scoring key at the end that you can flip to and see how compatible you are.

This is not a scored exercise.

The only scorecard is the mental one you create from a deeper understanding of how each partner feels about each answer they discuss with you.

I hope this book helps you to have a deep understanding of the amazing person you are considering spending the rest of your life with as a valuable relationship building tool.

Now it is time to get started! In chapter one, we will start with emotions and affection-related topics.

Amy Rose Herrick, ChFC

Christiansted, U.S. Virgin Islands

XV

PDF of the 25 Questions

If you would like to print off a copy of the 25 questions mentioned in the introduction to cut apart for drawing out of a container instead of the book order format, please use one of the links below.

You will find that each question in the book has additional helpful prompts you may want to refer to when having your discussion if you use the drawing at random method.

https://www.moneywithamyaudiobooks.com/knowingyourlifepartnerquestions

Chapter One

Emotional Questions

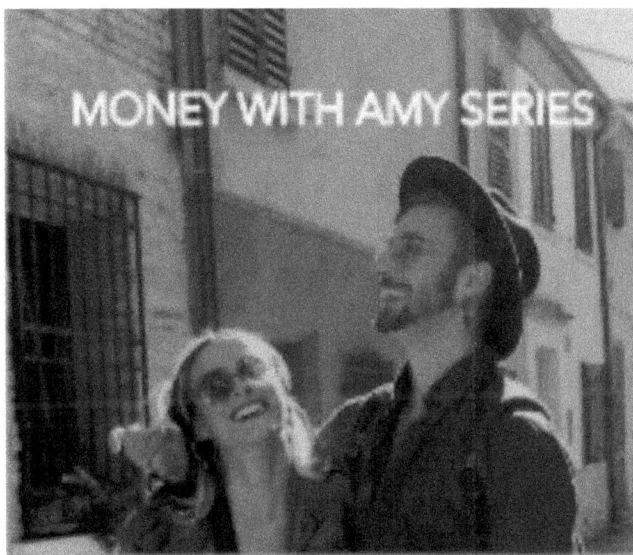

Question #1

Do I find you affectionate to the degree I expect from my life partner?

Name_____

If yes: What do you do that makes me feel special?

If not: What do you do that does not make me feel special?

Who do you think is responsible for your happiness in our relationship?

Describe a good marriage to you.

Do you know your love language?

(Partner #2 responses begin on the next page)

Question #1 (continued)

Do I find you affectionate to the degree I expect from my life partner?

Name_____

If yes: What do you do that makes me feel special?

If not: What do you do that does not make me feel special?

Who do you think is responsible for your happiness in our relationship?

Describe a good marriage to you.

Do you know your love language?

Question #2

Do you feel I truly listen to your ideas, point of view, dreams, and complaints?

Name: _____ Yes or No

If no:

What am I doing when you feel you are not being heard, ignored, or makes you feel misunderstood?

> Interrupt you.
>
> Tune you out.
>
> Ignore you.
>
> > Talk over you.
> >
> > Tell you what to do.

How do you react to conflict in a close relationship, giving examples?

Do you walk away to cool off and resume the conversation later in the day, ignore the person for how long, silent treatment for how long, throw things, scream, threaten, etc.?

Do resolution options for you include clergy or counseling with a third party, marriage retreats or others?

(Partner #2 responses begin on the next page)

Question #2 (continued)

Do you feel I truly listen to your ideas, point of view, dreams, and complaints?

Name: _____ Yes or No

If no:

What am I doing when you feel you are not being heard, ignored, or makes you feel misunderstood?

> Interrupt you.
>
> Tune you out.
>
> Ignore you.
>
> > Talk over you.
> >
> > Tell you what to do.

How do you react to conflict in a close relationship, giving examples?

> Do you walk away to cool off and resume the conversation later in the day, ignore the person for how long, silent treatment for how long, throw things, scream, threaten, etc.?
>
> Do resolution options for you include clergy or counseling with a third party, marriage retreats or others?

Question #3

Is there any personal activity or any existing personal relationship that you expect me to give up for this relationship, including pets?

Name: _____ Yes or No

   If yes:

      Why do you expect me to give this relationship up for you?

         Am I willing to give this relationship up for you?

      Why do you expect me to give this activity up for you?

      Am I willing to give this activity up for you?

         Is there room for compromise on this subject?

      What type of pets do you expect to have in our home?

      Do you have an allergy related to pets in the home?

      Other:

(Partner #2 responses begin on the next page)

Question #3 – continued

Is there any personal activity or any existing personal relationship that you expect me to give up for this relationship, including pets?

Name: _____ Yes or No

    If yes:

        Why do you expect me to give this relationship up for you?
            Am I willing to give this relationship up for you?

        Why do you expect me to give this activity up for you?
        Am I willing to give this activity up for you?

            Is there room for compromise on this subject?

        What type of pets do you expect to have in our home?
        Do you have an allergy related to pets in the home?
        Other:

Question #4

Do you believe in, or can you see yourself being able to forgive a partner for hurtful events such as an affair, conviction of a DUI, conviction for a crime, a breach of sexual trust, personal bankruptcy, children born out of a marriage that is not a part of your life, abortion, lying, etc.?

Name: _____ Response Yes or No

What are some examples of situations that would be so intolerable that you would end the relationship without forgiveness or compromise?

1. _____

2. _____

3. _____

(Partner #2 responses begin on the next page)

Question #4 continued

Do you believe in, or can you see yourself being able to forgive a partner for hurtful events such as an affair, conviction of a DUI, conviction for a crime, a breach of sexual trust, personal bankruptcy, children born out of a marriage that is not a part of your life, abortion, lying, etc.?

Name: _____ Response Yes or No

What are some examples of situations that would be so intolerable that you would end the relationship without forgiveness or compromise?

1. _____

2. _____

3. _____

In Chapter Two, we will explore relationship questions.

Chapter Two

Relationship Questions

MONEY WITH AMY SERIES

Question #5

Is it normal for you to snore, have a television, radio, fan, or other background noise on or bright light in the bedroom while sleeping?

Name: _____ Response Yes or No

If yes:

Do you snore?

Do you watch television in bed before falling asleep?

If you still fall asleep with the television, do you leave it on until morning?

Do you leave a radio on all night?

Do you have a fan or other appliance on all night?

Do you use any kind of sleep aid device that makes noise?

Do you require room darkening shades or drapes to block out all light to rest?

Is any noise or bright light coming through the window a problem for a light-sleeping partner?

Do you plan to sleep in the same bed with me?

What other sleep-related habits are normal for you?

(Partner #2 responses begin on the next page)

Question #5 continued

Is it normal for you to snore, have a television, radio, fan, or other background noise on or bright light in the bedroom while sleeping?

Name: _____ Response Yes or No

If yes:

Do you snore?

Do you watch television in bed before falling asleep?

If you still fall asleep with the television, do you leave it on until morning?

Do you leave a radio on all night?

Do you have a fan or other appliance on all night?

Do you use any kind of sleep aid device that makes noise?

Do you require room darkening shades or drapes to block out all light to rest?

Is any noise or bright light coming through the window a problem for a light-sleeping partner?

Do you plan to sleep in the same bed with me?

What other sleep-related habits are normal for you?

Question #6

Naming names, which of your friends, family or pets do I respect and want to spend time with, and which ones would I prefer not to spend any time with going forward?

Name: _____ Response

Persons or pets I willingly want to spend time with:

1._____

2._____

3._____

What are your relationship dynamics with these individuals?

Do not make me ever spend time with them again if I or we can figure out a way to avoid it:

1._____

2._____

3._____

What are your relationship dynamics with these individuals?

(Partner #2 responses begin on the next page)

Question #6 continued

Naming names, which of your friends, family or pets do I respect and want to spend time with, and which ones would I prefer not to spend any time with going forward?

Name: _____ Response

Persons or pets I willingly want to spend time with:

1._____

2._____

3._____

What are your relationship dynamics with these individuals?

Do not make me ever spend time with them again if I or we can figure out a way to avoid it:

1._____

2._____

3._____

What are your relationship dynamics with these individuals?

Question #7

What do you do in your free time? Am I expected or required to be a part of this activity? How much time is required?

Name: _____ Response Yes or No

    Examples:

        Reading

        Video, internet, or cell phone games

        Volunteer

        Club memberships

        Hobbies

        Exercise

        Sports activities

        Church activities

        Other

(Partner #2 responses begin on the next page)

Question #7 continued

What do you do in your free time? Am I expected or required to be a part of this activity? How much time is required?

Name: _____ Response Yes or No

    Examples:

        Reading

        Video, internet, or cell phone games

        Volunteer

        Club memberships

        Hobbies

        Exercise

        Sports activities

        Church activities

        Other

In Chapter Three, we will explore medical histories and health issues.

Chapter Three

Medical Questions

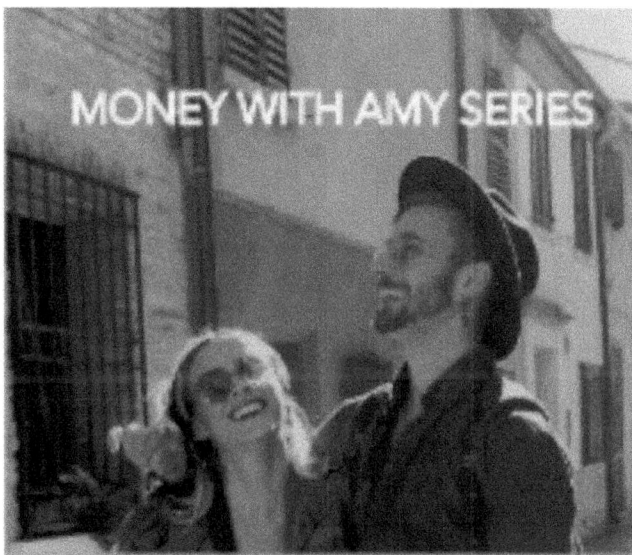

Question #8

Have we fully disclosed our complete health histories and practices?

Name: _____ Response Yes or No

Examples:

Every current medication I am on for physical illness?

Every current medication I am on for mental illnesses?

Do I get yearly physicals, Pap smears, mammograms, prostate checks, bloodwork, diabetic checks, vision care, tooth cleaning, etc.?

How serious am I about maintaining my health with regular exercise, eating habits, alcohol consumption, etc.?

Past minor and major surgeries?

Known medical conditions.?

Suspected medical conditions or upcoming surgeries?

Genetic conditions that run in my family?

Past mental illness episodes?

Drug abuse issues or history?

Alcohol abuse issues or history?

Nicotine use past or present in any form?

Do I vape?

Do I do snuff?

Domestic abuse history as victim?

Domestic abuse history as instigator?

Sexual abuse history?

Rape survivor?

Other?

(Partner #2 responses begin on the next page)

Question #8 continued

Have we fully disclosed our complete health histories and practices?

Name: _____ Response Yes or No

> Examples:
>
> Every current medication I am on for physical illness?
>
> Every current medication I am on for mental illnesses?
>
> Do I get yearly physicals, Pap smears, mammograms, prostate checks, bloodwork, diabetic checks, vision care, tooth cleaning, etc.?
>
> How serious am I about maintaining my health with regular exercise, eating habits, alcohol consumption, etc.?
>
> Past minor and major surgeries?
>
> Known medical conditions.?
>
> Suspected medical conditions or upcoming surgeries?
>
> Genetic conditions that run in my family?
>
> Past mental illness episodes?
>
> Drug abuse issues or history?
>
> Alcohol abuse issues or history?
>
> Nicotine use past or present in any form?
>
> Do I vape?
>
> Do I do snuff?
>
> Domestic abuse history as victim?
>
> Domestic abuse history as instigator?
>
> Sexual abuse history?

Rape survivor?

Other?

Question #9

Do I have health, air ambulance, critical illness, cancer, disability, and/or long-term care insurance in case I become ill or injured and cannot work?

Name_____ Responses Yes or No

How much of the earnings will your disability policy replace?

Does your policy pay a fixed amount for critical illness or cancer?

How long do any systematic benefits last?

Is coverage privately owned or through your employment?

If No:

Why do you not currently have adequate health or air ambulance insurance?

What are you doing now to secure adequate health or air ambulance insurance?

Why do you not currently have disability or long-term care insurance?

What are you doing now to secure disability or long-term care insurance?

How do you plan to pay for your medical treatment without insurance?

How do you plan to meet debt and living expenses if you are injured or ill and cannot earn an income?

(Partner #2 responses begin on the next page)

Question #9 continued

Do you have health, air ambulance, critical illness, cancer, disability and/or long-term care insurance in case I become ill or injured and cannot work?

Name_____ Responses Yes or No

How much of the earnings will your disability policy replace?

Does your policy pay a fixed amount for critical illness or cancer?

How long do any systematic benefits last?

Is coverage privately owned or through your employment?

If No:

Why do you not currently have adequate health or air ambulance insurance?

What are you doing now to secure adequate health or air ambulance insurance?

Why do you not currently have disability or long-term care insurance?

What are you doing now to secure disability or long-term care insurance?

How do you plan to pay for your medical treatment without insurance?

How do you plan to meet debt and living expenses if you are injured or ill and cannot earn an income?

In Chapter Four, we will explore financial issues that will affect your ability to maintain or accumulate wealth.

Chapter Four

Financial Questions

MONEY WITH AMY SERIES

Question #10

Are you prepared to give up your job and/or volunteer activities to relocate with me if I am offered a career opportunity in a location far from our present home or from either family?

Name: _____ Response Yes or No

If no, why not?

If yes or maybe:

      Would you only relocate to a city or metro area atmosphere?

      Would you be open to relocating to a rural or country atmosphere?

      Would you relocate outside of our current state?

      Would you need to secure a job before moving to a new location?

      Would you move to a foreign country? Temporarily for up to _____ years or less? Longer?

      Are you open to moving where English or _____ is not the only language spoken?

      If we were unable to travel to see family and friends often, would this be a deal-breaker?

(Partner #2 responses begin on the next page)

Question #10 continued

Are you prepared to give up your job and/or volunteer activities to relocate with me if I am offered a career opportunity in a location far from our present home or from either family?

Name: _____ Response Yes or No

If no, why not?

If yes or maybe:

> Would you only relocate to a city or metro area atmosphere?
>
> Would you be open to relocating to a rural or country atmosphere?
>
> Would you relocate outside of our current state?
>
> Would you need to secure a job before moving to a new location?
>
> Would you move to a foreign country? Temporarily for up to _____ years or less? Longer?
>
> Are you open to moving where English or _____is not the only language spoken?
>
> If we were unable to travel to see family and friends often, would this be a deal-breaker?

Question #11

How many months or years have you drawn unemployment in your working career?

Name: _____ Response Yes or No

    If you have drawn unemployment benefits in the past:

        Describe the circumstances.

        How long were you unemployed?

      Do you see a layoff or downsizing in your career soon?

      Do you have periods of time that would cause you to routinely seek unemployment benefits seasonally for example?

      Do you plan to collect unemployment for part of every year?

      When drawing unemployment, how do you plan to make up the income shortfall until reemployed?

      What happens to your health insurance during this time of unemployment?

Idea: You may want to pull your individual Social Security reports from https://www.SSA.gov to see if you have earned enough credits to qualify for disability benefits for you from this resource based on your work and earnings history.

The disability component that involves determination of benefits process can take up to two years to move through the approval steps and to receive your first benefit payment… if you qualify. You would need to fill the financial gap in the interim.

There is a separate section to see if you qualify for survivor benefits in the event of premature death that could help support a surviving spouse and/or your minor aged children.

If you were married for more than 10 years, there could be other retirement benefits you could qualify for that may be higher than your own.

(Partner #2 responses begin on the next page)

Question #11 continued

How many months or years have you drawn unemployment in your working career?

Name: _____ Response Yes or No

      If you have drawn unemployment benefits in the past:

          Describe the circumstances.

          How long were you unemployed?

     Do you see a layoff or downsizing in your career soon?

     Do you have periods of time that would cause you to routinely seek unemployment benefits seasonally for example?

     Do you plan to collect unemployment for part of every year?

     When drawing unemployment, how do you plan to make up the income shortfall until reemployed?

     What happens to your health insurance during this time of unemployment?

Idea: You may want to pull your individual Social Security reports from https://www.SSA.gov to see if you have earned enough credits to qualify for disability benefits for you from this resource based on your work and earnings history.

The disability component that involves determination of benefits process can take up to two years to move through the approval steps and to receive your first benefit payment… if you qualify. You would need to fill the financial gap in the interim.

There is a separate section to see if you qualify for survivor benefits in the event of premature death that could help support a surviving spouse and/or your minor aged children.

If you were married for more than 10 years, there could be other retirement benefits you could qualify for that may be higher than your own.

Question #12

If you needed to pay $10,000 - $100,000 for something extra or unexpected, which options would you choose to pay for it (number in order)?

Name: _____ Response

    ___Get a short-term part-time job to earn the money

    ___ Sell my _____ (name asset)

    ___ Ask my parents/friends/relatives for the money

    ___ Use money I have in savings.

            $_____ current balance.

    ___ I would increase my debt load on credit cards.

            Unused credit available $_____

    ___ I expect my partner to help pay for it or pay for it

    from their resources.

    ___ Other, explain: _____

(Partner #2 responses begin on the next page)

Question #12 continued

If you needed to pay $10,000 - $100,000 for something extra or unexpected, which options would you choose to pay for it (number in order)?

Name: _____ Response

___Get a short-term part-time job to earn the money

___ Sell my _____ (name asset)

___ Ask my parents/friends/relatives for the money

___ Use money I have in savings.

$_____ current balance.

___ I would increase my debt load on credit cards.

Unused credit available $_____

___ I expect my partner to help pay for it or pay for it

from their resources.

___ Other, explain: _____

Question #13

If you could only afford to get married in a simple ceremony costing no more than $500-2,000 for everything with no honeymoon, no big guest list, no fancy cake, or other extras, would you still get married to me?

Name: _____ Response Yes or No

If no:

Is this because you want to wait until we can have a lavish ceremony?

Social pressure from family?

What are your other reasons for waiting?

Please describe what you envision our wedding and honeymoon to be like.

What is the budget you expect us to pay for our wedding festivities, clothing, rings, church, refreshments, honeymoon, etc.?

Budget you have in mind
$_____

(Partner #2 responses begin on the next page)

Question #13 continued

If you could only afford to get married in a simple ceremony costing no more than $500-2,000 for everything with no honeymoon, no big guest list, no fancy cake, or other extras, would you still get married to me?

Name: _____ Response Yes or No

If no:

        Is this because you want to wait until we can have a lavish ceremony?

        Social pressure from family?

        What are your other reasons for waiting?

        Please describe what you envision our wedding and honeymoon to be like.

        What is the budget you expect us to pay for our wedding festivities, clothing, rings, church, refreshments, honeymoon, etc.?

        Budget you have in mind

        $_____

Question #14

Have you disclosed to me a complete list of every financial obligation you are aware of?

Name: _____ Response Yes or No

Does this include:

All your existing debt balances including credit cards $_____

Motorcycle or car loans? $_____

Mortgage on a home, other property, or time-share? $_____

Any unpaid judgments against you? $_____

Any potential pending litigations? $_____

Student loans – current or in arrears? $_____

Child support – current or in arrears? $_____

Alimony - current or in arrears? $_____

Unpaid loans from family members? $_____

Unpaid loans from friends? $_____

Other? $_____

Tax liens or balances due on taxes from prior years?   Yes or No

Year ____ $_____

Year ____ $_____

Year ____ $_____

Total estimated debt $_____

(Partner #2 responses begin on the next page)

Question #14 continued

Have you disclosed to me a complete list of every financial obligation you are aware of?

Name: _____ Response Yes or No

Does this include:

All your existing debt balances including credit cards $_____

Motorcycle or car loans? $_____

Mortgage on a home, other property, or time-share? $_____

Any unpaid judgments against you? $_____

Any potential pending litigations? $_____

Student loans – current or in arrears? $_____

Child support – current or in arrears? $_____

Alimony - current or in arrears? $_____

Unpaid loans from family members? $_____

Unpaid loans from friends? $_____

Other? $_____

Tax liens or balances due on taxes from prior years? Yes or No

Year _____ $_____

Year _____ $_____

Year _____ $_____

Total estimated debt $_____

Question #15

Do our ideas, beliefs, and actions about life insurance, spending, and saving money for the future align perfectly, or are we conducting our financial affairs now with vastly different philosophies?

Name: _____ Responses

Suggestions for life insurance

$_____ annual gross earnings x 20 years   =$_____
Insurance I own $_____

> Who are your current primary and contingent beneficiaries?
>
> Will you change your beneficiaries after we are married, or will all primary and contingent beneficiaries remain the same on existing coverage?
>
> Will you be securing additional life insurance with your partner as primary beneficiary?
>
> > Why or why not?

Suggestion for disability coverage monthly earnings

$_____x 70% = $_____ $_____

Suggestion for critical illness coverage annual earnings

$_____ x 2 = $_____ $_____

Suggestion for long term care coverage varies

$_____ X__ = $_____ $_____

Monthly savings deposits left on deposit untouched $_____
Balance now $_____

Monthly savings for short term purchases $_____
Balance now $_____

Monthly deposits for retirement $_____

Balance now $_____

Other financial goals you are funding _____ $_____
Balance now $_____

Do you share any accounts with another person?

    Why?

    Will this change after we are married?

Will we open a new joint account or keep the finances separate?

How will we share/divide/allocate joint household expenses?

If one partner owns the home you are both living in, what will happen to the non-owner spouse's residency should the owner die?

Other?

(Partner #2 responses begin on the next page)

Question #15 continued

Do our ideas, beliefs, and actions about life insurance, spending, and saving money for the future align perfectly, or are we conducting our financial affairs now with vastly different philosophies?

Name: _____ Responses

Suggestions for life insurance

$_____ annual gross earnings x 20 years   =$_____
Insurance I own $_____

> Who are your current primary and contingent beneficiaries?
>
> Will you change your beneficiaries after we are married, or will all primary and contingent beneficiaries remain the same on existing coverage?
>
> Will you be securing additional life insurance with your partner as primary beneficiary?
>
> > Why or why not?

Suggestion for disability coverage monthly earnings

$_____x 70% = $_____ $_____

Suggestion for critical illness coverage annual earnings

$_____ x 2   = $_____ $_____

Suggestion for long term care coverage varies

$_____ X__ = $_____ $_____

Monthly savings deposits left on deposit untouched $_____
Balance now $_____

Monthly savings for short term purchases $_____
Balance now $_____

Monthly deposits for retirement $_____

Balance now $_____

Other financial goals you are funding _____ $_____
Balance now $_____

Do you share any accounts with another person?

     Why?

     Will this change after we are married?

Will we open a new joint account or keep the finances separate?

How will we share/divide/allocate joint household expenses?

If one partner owns the home you are both living in, what will happen to the non-owner spouse's residency should the owner die?

Other?

Question #16

Before asking this question, each person must present and share a complete credit report, including their current credit score.

      800 or Higher- Exceptional

      740-799 Very Dependable

      670-739 Good Score

      580-669 Some Approved

      579 and below- very Risky

Name: _____ Responses

Is your report a current accounting of your credit record? *Hint: Look on your credit card website for free access to scores.*

How and when are you going to correct any negative comments and/or repay any unpaid claims against you on the report?

Have you ever used other names or aliases? Why?

Do you qualify for credit easily now?

What is your FICO Score? _____

(Partner #2 responses begin on the next page)

Question #16 continued

Before asking this question, each person must present and share a complete credit report, including their current credit score.

800 or Higher- Exceptional

740-799 Very Dependable

670-739 Good Score

580-669 Some Approved

579 and below- very Risky

Name: _____ Responses

Is your report a current accounting of your credit record? *Hint: Look on your credit card website for free access to scores.*

How and when are you going to correct any negative comments and/or repay any unpaid claims against you on the report?

Have you ever used other names or aliases? Why?

Do you qualify for credit easily now?

What is your FICO Score? _____

Question #17

Have you used or received public assistance resources, including housing, medical care, food stamps, income, etc.?

Name: _____ Response

If so, describe the circumstances and duration of time you needed assistance.

What programs are you utilizing now?

        Rent reduced housing?

        Food stamps?

        Free lunches for children at school?

        Utilities assistance?

        Medicaid health coverage?

        Other?

Will you lose benefits at marriage?

If yes, what is your plan to cover the gap in benefits or income because of getting married?

(Partner #2 responses begin on the next page)

Question #17 continued

Have you used or received public assistance resources, including housing, medical care, food stamps, income, etc.?

Name: _____ Response

If so, describe the circumstances and duration of time you needed assistance.

What programs are you utilizing now?

       Rent reduced housing?

       Food stamps?

       Free lunches for children at school?

       Utilities assistance?

       Medicaid health coverage?

       Other?

Will you lose benefits at marriage?

If yes, what is your plan to cover the gap in benefits or income because of getting married?

In Chapter Five, we will talk about your family related dynamics and expectations.

Chapter Five

Family Matters Questions

Question #18

Do you already have children conceived in or out of marriage?

Name: _____ Response Yes or No

If yes, be specific per child in terms of:

a) What are the names and ages of the children?
b) Where do they live now?
c) Where will they be living in the future?
d) What kind of child support is received or required to be paid monthly?
e) Is child support paid consistently or in arrears?
f) Have you firmly established paternity?
g) What are the current custody and visitation arrangements?
h) Do you expect custody or visitation arrangements to change?
i) Do you claim the children for income taxes? Every year or alternate years?
j) Do you pay for health insurance for the children?
k) Do you have other support obligations related to the children that are not included in child support, such as long summer vacations that you need to pay for childcare when working, annual holiday travel airfare expenses, piano lessons, etc.?
l) Does your child have any known addiction issues such as alcohol or drug abuse?
m) Does your child have a gambling or gaming addiction?
n) Does your child have any mental or physical disabilities?
o) Are you helping to pay for legal issues for your children's crime-related events?
p) Are you supporting any adult children with specific expenses or regular cash gifts?
q) How is your working relationship with the child's other parent?
    a. Combative
    b. Cooperative
    c. Distance related visitation issues are a problem.
    d. We have no distance related visitation issues.
    e. I must go to court often for issue resolution.
    f. We can easily converse; we are civil and attend extended family events together.
    g. It is best if we are not in the same location at the same time.
    h. If asked, I will help this person with anything.
    i. They will die if they think I will save them.

j.   They constantly ask for or demand more money.

k.   I help financially when asked when I can.
l.   Other.

(Partner #2 responses begin on the next page

Question #18 continued

Do you already have children conceived in or out of marriage?

Name: _____ Response Yes or No

If yes, be specific per child in terms of:

a) What are the names and ages of the children?
b) Where do they live now?
c) Where will they be living in the future?
d) What kind of child support is received or required to be paid monthly?
e) Is child support paid consistently or in arrears?
f) Have you firmly established paternity?
g) What are the current custody and visitation arrangements?
h) Do you expect custody or visitation arrangements to change?
i) Do you claim the children for income taxes? Every year or alternate years?
j) Do you pay for health insurance for the child?
k) Do you have other support obligations related to the children that are not included in child support, such as long summer vacations that you need to pay for childcare when working, annual holiday travel airfare expenses, piano lessons, etc.?
l) Does your child have any known addiction issues such as alcohol or drug abuse?
m) Does your child have a gambling or gaming addiction?
n) Does your child have any mental or physical disabilities?
o) Are you helping to pay for legal issues for your children's crime-related events?
p) Are you supporting any adult children with specific expenses or regular cash gifts?
q) How is your working relationship with the child's other parent?
    m. Combative
    n. Cooperative
    o. Distance related visitation issues are a problem.
    p. We have no distance related visitation issues.
    q. I must go to court often for issue resolution.
    r. We can easily converse; we are civil and attend extended family events together.
    s. It is best if we are not in the same location at the same time.
    t. If asked, I will help this person with anything.
    u. They will die if they think I will save them.

v.   They constantly ask for or demand more money.
w.   I help financially when asked when I can.
x.   Other.

Question #19

Do you plan on conceiving, using surrogacy, or adopting a child or children as a part of our future together?

Name: _____ Response Yes or No

If the answer is yes:

a) When do you want to start a family?
b) How will we pay for the birth expenses?
c) How will we pay for the new baby's needs?
d) If you expect a parent to come help with a new birth for a time, which parent will come help, and for how long? Will they live in the home with us during that time or stay elsewhere and come and go as needed?
e) What methods of contraception will we use if applicable?
f) If an unplanned pregnancy occurred to us, do you agree or disagree with abortion as an option open for discussion?
g) Will both parents continue to work full time after the children arrive?
h) Who do you expect to be the primary caregiver?
i) If you were sterilized, are you willing or able to have it reversed?
j) Is domestic or international adoption an option you would consider?
k) Are donor eggs, donor sperm, or surrogate pregnancy any options you would consider?
l) Do you expect to raise our children with a specific religious, educational base in our home?
m) Who is responsible for smelly diaper changes?
n) How do you feel about breastfeeding?
o) How do you feel about bottle feeding?
p) Who do you expect to do the overnight feedings and diaper changes?
q) Would you use cloth diapers to save money, for environmental reasons, or only disposable ones?
r) Do you agree or disagree with male circumcision?

(Partner #2 responses begin on the next page)

Question #19 continued

Do you plan on conceiving, using surrogacy, or adopting a child or children as a part of our future together?

Name: _____ Response Yes or No

   If the answer is yes:

   a) When do you want to start a family?
   b) How will we pay for the birth expenses?
   c) How will we pay for the new baby's needs?
   d) If you expect a parent to come help with a new birth for a time, which parent will come help, and for how long? Will they live in the home with us during that time or stay elsewhere and come and go as needed?
   e) What methods of contraception will we use if applicable?
   f) If an unplanned pregnancy occurred to us, do you agree or disagree with abortion as an option open for discussion?
   g) Will both parents continue to work full time after the children arrive?
   h) Who do you expect to be the primary caregiver?
   i) If you were sterilized, are you willing or able to have it reversed?
   j) Is domestic or international adoption an option you would consider?
   k) Are donor eggs, donor sperm, or surrogate pregnancy any options you would consider?
   l) Do you expect to raise our children with a specific religious, educational base in our home?
   m) Who is responsible for smelly diaper changes?
   n) How do you feel about breastfeeding?
   o) How do you feel about bottle feeding?
   p) Who do you expect to do the overnight feedings and diaper changes?
   q) Would you use cloth diapers to save money, for environmental reasons, or only disposable ones?
   r) Do you agree or disagree with male circumcision?

Question #20

What do my family or friends do that annoys you?

Be specific and provide examples.

Name: _____ Responses

Example ideas:

Holidays- Is there an activity we do that you do not understand we have as perhaps a tradition?

Social Events?

Gifting practices?

Cleanliness, poor housekeeping skills, hoarding, etc.?

Derogatory, offensive, or upsetting nicknames?

Smoking, drug abuse, alcohol addiction, gambling, etc.?

Political related rants?

Other?

(Partner #2 responses begin on the next page)

Question #20 continued

What do my family or friends do that annoys you?

Be specific and provide examples.

Name: _____ Responses

Example ideas:

Holidays- Is there an activity we do that you do not understand we have as perhaps a tradition?

Social Events?

Gifting practices?

Cleanliness, poor housekeeping skills, hoarding, etc.?

Derogatory, offensive, or upsetting nicknames?

Smoking, drug abuse, alcohol addiction, gambling, etc.?

Political related rants?

Other?

Question #21

Is either of us concerned about becoming a primary caregiver, guardian, or Power of Attorney for our parents, other minor-aged children in the family tree, or from close friends, or adult disabled siblings, or an incompetent family member of any age?

Name: _____ Response Yes or No

If yes:

> Who is this person?
>
> How do you envision you will need to help?
>
> In what capacity will you need to serve his/her needs?
>
> When do you expect this to happen?
>
> Do you expect him/her to live with you during that time?
>
> Will you have to move to manage this role?
>
> Will they need to be moved to enable you to take on this role?
>
> Will other family members share this responsibility with you?

How will any loss of income be handled if you must reduce hours or quit your job to manage the care of a loved one in need?

Do you have a Power of Attorney now for this person in your possession?

Do you have a Medical Power of Attorney for this person in your possession?

If they have a trust, are your names as a Trustee to manage trust assets when needed?

(Partner #2 responses on the next page)

Question #21 continued

Is either of us concerned about becoming a primary caregiver, guardian, or Power of Attorney for our parents, other minor-aged children in the family tree or from close friends, or adult disabled siblings, or an incompetent family member of any age?

Name: _____ Response Yes or No

If yes:

Who is this person?

How do you envision you will need to help?

In what capacity will you need to serve his/her needs?

When do you expect this to happen?

Do you expect him/her to live with you during that time?

Will you have to move to manage this role?

Will they need to be moved to enable you to take on this role?

Will other family members share this responsibility with you?

How will any loss of income be handled if you must reduce hours or quit your job to manage the care of a loved one in need?

Do you have a Power of Attorney now for this person in your possession?

Do you have a Medical Power of Attorney for this person in your possession?

If they have a trust, are your names as a Trustee to manage trust assets when needed?

In Chapter Six, we will explore issues that relate to your new household needs and management of day-to-day tasks.

Chapter Six

Household Management Question

Question #22

Describe your expectations for the household management.

Name: _____ Responses

Examples:

> What is your expectation of any gender or title related roles in our household such as wife/husband/partner?

> Who do you envision doing the following?
>
> > Washing dishes
> >
> > Cooking meals
> >
> > Laundry
> >
> > Vacuuming and sweeping floors
> >
> > Pet care, including food, grooming and vet visits, etc.

> How much dust or clutter is acceptable to you?
>
> Are you physically able to do heavy work like lifting furniture, lawn work, or other home maintenance items, or must these be hired out?
>
> Is homeownership important to you?
>
> Who handles landscaping and lawn type care?
>
> Pool care?
>
> Do you clean your own home, or do you have maid services?
>
> How often should the floor be mopped?
>
> How often should the shower be cleaned?
>
> How often should the sheets on the bed be changed?
>
> Other:

(Partner #2 responses begin on the next page)

Describe your expectations for the household management.

Name: _____ Responses

Examples:

> What is your expectation of any gender or title related roles in our household such as wife/husband/partner?

> Who do you envision doing the following?
>> Washing dishes
>>
>> Cooking meals
>>
>> Laundry
>>
>> Vacuuming and sweeping floors
>>
>> Pet care, including food, grooming and vet visits etc.

> How much dust or clutter is acceptable to you?

> Are you physically able to do heavy work like lifting furniture, lawn work, or other home maintenance items, or must these be hired out?

> Is homeownership important to you?

> Who handles landscaping and lawn type care?

> Pool care?

> Do you clean your own home, or do you have maid services?

> How often should the floor be mopped?

> How often should the shower be cleaned?

> How often should the sheets on the bed be changed?

> Other:

In Chapter Seven, we will explore your faith or religious based expectations.

Chapter Seven

Religious Question

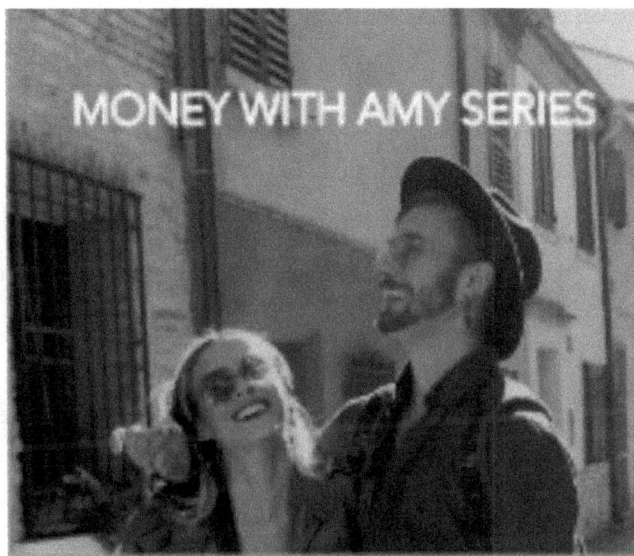

MONEY WITH AMY SERIES

Question #23

What is your plan for meeting your religious or other belief system needs?

Name: _____ Religious affiliation Yes or No

If you have a religious affiliation:

What is the name of your faith? _____

How do you visualize my part in your religious activities?

How do you visualize honoring your beliefs as a couple?

How do you visualize us honoring your beliefs in our home?

How do you visualize us honoring your beliefs if children are involved in our home?

What do you use for reference materials for your beliefs?

Would there be any reason either of us would not be accepted in a religious house of worship as a couple?

Are there specific religious traditions you plan to follow I should know about?

Do you plan to join me in my faith or religious activities if they are different than yours?

Etc.

(Partner #2 responses begin on the next page)

What is your plan for meeting your religious or other belief system needs?

Name: _____ Religious affiliation Yes or No

If you have a religious affiliation:

What is the name of your faith? _____

How do you visualize my part in your religious activities?

How do you visualize honoring your beliefs as a couple?

How do you visualize us honoring your beliefs in our home?

How do you visualize us honoring your beliefs if children are involved in our home?

What do you use for reference materials for your beliefs?

Would there be any reason either of us would not be accepted in a religious house of worship as a couple?

Are there specific religious traditions you plan to follow I should know about?

Do you plan to join me in my faith or religious activities if they are different than yours?

Etc.

In Chapter Eight, we will feel perhaps a little uneasy or vulnerable as we discuss our sexuality expectations and preferences.

Chapter Eight
Sexual Question

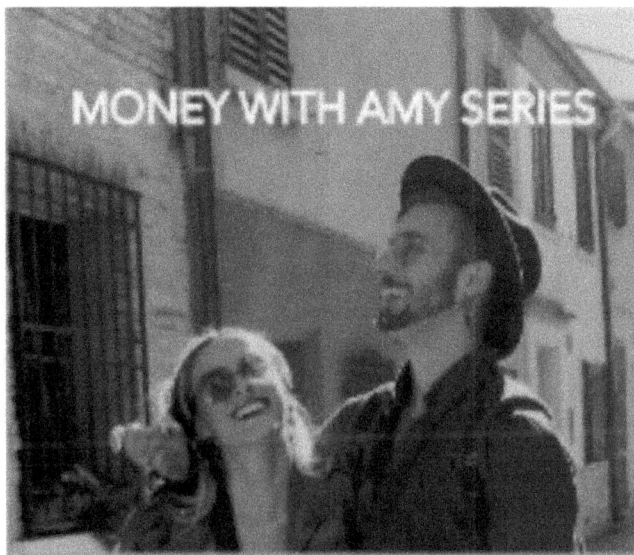

Question #24

Have you had one or more sexual partners before me, and do you have specific sexual expectations to be met in our future?

Name: _____ Response Yes or No

If yes:

How many?

Do your sexual experiences include more than one sexual orientation?

Did you contract any sexual disease in a prior relationship?

Do you have current AIDS, HIV, STD testing results to share with me?

If not, are you willing to obtain AID, HIV or other STD testing and share your certificate of health results with me?

Can I comfortably and openly discuss sexual needs, preferences, dislikes, and fears inside and outside of the bedroom citing specific examples of likes and dislikes?

What frequency is a healthy sex life to you weekly/monthly?

Are there any sexual expectations after marriage for the inclusion of sex toys, swinging, other partners, etc.?

What are your personal hygiene practices or expectation before or after sex?

Other?

(Partner #2 responses begin on the next page)

Have you had one or more sexual partners before me, and do you have specific sexual expectations to be met in our future?

Name: _____ Response Yes or No

If yes:

How many?

Do your sexual experiences include more than one sexual orientation?

Did you contract any sexual disease in a prior relationship?

Do you have current AIDS, HIV, STD testing results to share with me?

     If not, are you willing to obtain AID, HIV or other STD testing and share your certificate of health results with me?

Can I comfortably and openly discuss sexual needs, preferences, dislikes, and fears inside and outside of the bedroom citing specific examples of likes and dislikes?

What frequency is a healthy sex life to you weekly/monthly?

Are there any sexual expectations after marriage for the inclusion of sex toys, swinging, other partners, etc.?

What are your personal hygiene practices or expectation before or after sex?

Other?

In our final Chapter Nine, we will discuss whether a prenuptial agreement will be completed with the help of separate legal counsel.

Chapter Nine
Prenuptial Question

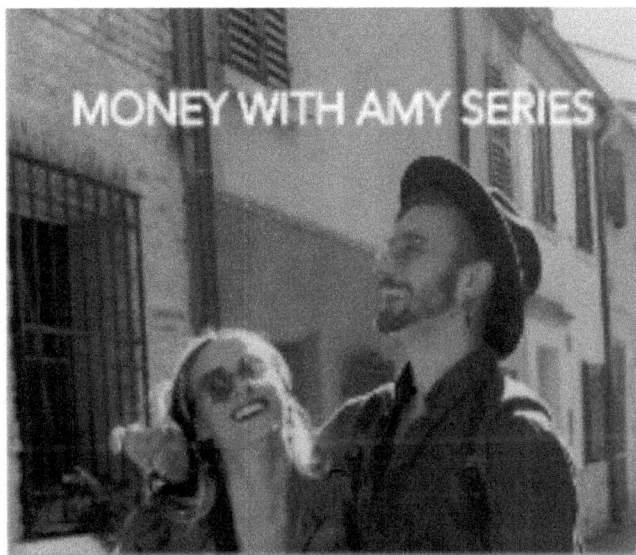

Question #25

Does either of us expect to engage an attorney to draw up and formally implement a prenuptial agreement before we are married?

Name: _____ Response Yes or No

If yes, what are some things we are thinking about:

Comingling our household obligations?

Commingling our assets?

Commingling our income resources?

Filing taxes as a couple for joint tax liability or filing separately for individual liability?

Hint: Check current local jurisdiction and Federal laws for any special requirements.

Commingling future joint debts?

Who will pay ongoing household expenses?

How will housing be owned?

How will vehicles be owned?

How will other property be owned?

Inheritances for any children born or adopted prior to this union will be _____

Inheritances for any children born or adopted in this union will be

_____

(This discussion is continued for 2nd person on the next page)

Question #25 continued

Does either of us expect to engage an attorney to draw up and formally implement a prenuptial agreement before we are married?

Name: _____ Response Yes or No

If yes, what are some things we are thinking about:

Comingling our household obligations?

Commingling our assets?

Commingling our income resources?

Filing taxes as a couple for joint tax liability or filing separately for individual liability?

Hint: Check current local jurisdiction and Federal laws for any special requirements.

Commingling future joint debts?

Who will pay ongoing household expenses?

How will housing be owned?

How will vehicles be owned?

How will other property be owned?

Inheritances for any children born or adopted prior to this union will be _____

Inheritances for any children born or adopted in this union will be

_____

Afterthoughts: We have a big problem. We are at an impasse.

Some of you may be hurt by a revelation because of the probing or deeply personal questions asked.

Perhaps you found you have very different ideas on a topic you had assumed you would be compatible with.

Whatever happens, you feel stuck on a divisive issue or two, and now what should you do?

You should go to the next step to seek a qualified, trusted resource to help you further discuss the issue to see where you can compromise and where you cannot.

Not agreeing on everything is not always a relationship-ending event, but it could be if it is a non-negotiable item for either partner.

You could seek out help from a pastor, priest, other counselor-type, clergy, member. Perhaps you choose a professional counselor, psychologist, medical professional, or other qualified people who can help give you more clarity or insight may be helpful. You are not right or wrong to feel the way you do about any issue. It is a part of who you are.

Who can help answer your questions, address your fears of the unknown or help you to understand the other person's perspective better? Who can help you reach a compromise?

In some situations, you may ultimately decide to let this relationship go if you cannot see a future together as being the one you seek. Who will be your support system?

Not addressing the issue that is threatening your future happiness is not a solution. It is generally an unwise decision to ignore something. Ignoring an issue is often called "the elephant in the room" syndrome. Avoiding mentioning the elephant like it will suddenly disappear is not the same as trying to find a solution before the elephant takes over everything and everyone's attention in the whole house.

I wish you the best of times as you invest so much of your future into each other.

Congratulations on knowing your chosen partner better than ever before.

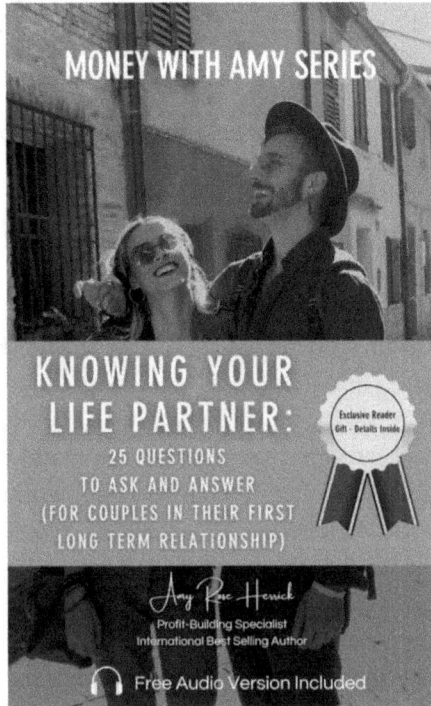

THANK YOU FOR READING MY BOOK!

As a thank-you, we'd love to send you a free bonus book- not for sale anywhere else. Just email us at INFO@AmyRoseHerrick.com with "Bonus Book Request" in the subject line. You'll receive your exclusive gift directly by email.

Loved the book? We'd be grateful for your honest review on Amazon— but the bonus is yours either way.

ACKNOWLEDGMENTS

Without the support of many over the years, I could not be the person I am today. I know I will forget to thank someone, but it was not my intention to do so.

To my family, who do not always understand me, but love me anyway, you mean the world to me.

To friends and colleagues who support my professional talents and literary dreams, I wish you continued success in your endeavors.

To my talented VA team who helped me to have the finished content in print form, may your dreams come true too.

To the online writing groups from around the world on Zoom meetings where we encouraged each other in the manuscript writing processes, I did it and so can you!

To my clients and live audiences who helped me learn so much about this topic with the sharing of their life stories of successes and failures for me to give guidance to you today, thank you for allowing me to have a positive impact on your lives.

To my mentors, I promise to pay it forward.

To my draft version reviewers with all the helpful suggestions and encouragement to get this finished quickly, you will see many of your suggestions incorporated.

And finally, to all the ones behind the scenes we take for granted that make websites, online ordering, eBooks, printing, shipping, and delivery possible for us all…a heartfelt thank you for being a part of my world every day.

About the Author

Amy Rose Herrick, ChFC, is an extraordinary author and financial expert dedicated to transforming lives while empowering individuals and businesses to achieve unparalleled financial success.

Some remarkable solutions take 15 minutes or less to understand and implement.

Her expertise shines brightest creating personalized, comprehensive plans that streamline costs, provide peace of mind, and secure wealth for future generations.

Bid farewell to financial stress while embracing your legacy that will endure the test of time.

Amy, your personal wealth building guide, unleashes the power within your resources.

Complex resource management problems are transformed into easy step by step solutions.

Using groundbreaking methodology, Amy empowers individuals, business owners, and families alike.

Entrepreneurs flock to Amy for clear, actionable tutorials on building more profitable businesses. Under her guidance, ventures can thrive like never before, unlocking their true potential for financial success.

As a fiduciary, Chartered Financial Consultant, and tax professional, Amy has mastered the art of optimizing resources.

Yet, her achievements do not stop there. She is a #1 Best Selling Author, captivating speaker, talented artist, and a dedicated force in community service.

With over three decades of experience, including more than 25 years in the Securities industry, Amy possesses an impressive array of qualifications and expertise. She equips you with the tools to experience lasting financial freedom, providing a transformative journey unlike any other.

In 2024, be prepared for the launch of a series of game-changing books and captivating YouTube videos titled "Money With Amy."

Her dynamic and easy-to-understand content will empower you to strategically structure your resources for the benefit of your family and businesses.

Amy Rose Herrick's list of remarkable accomplishments is truly awe-inspiring. From being named Small Business of the Year to being a #1 Best Selling Author, a National Geographic 'Chasing Genius' Finalist, and even teaching a gorilla named Max, Amy's impact is undeniable.

Clients can expect an unforgettable, life-changing experience with Amy Rose Herrick, one that simply cannot be replicated elsewhere.

Currently residing by the sea in the breathtaking US Virgin Islands, Amy continues to live a life of abundance while sharing her wealth of knowledge with the world.

For Additional Information & Resources

Visit Amy's website: **www.AmyRoseHerrick.com**

Email: **Amy@AmyRoseHerrick.com**

Book a 15-minute Zoom based discovery call to discuss becoming a client for comprehensive financial planning or business profit building assistance at:

https://calendly.com/amyroseherrick/15min

Follow Amy on Facebook

https://www.facebook.com/AmyRoseHerrickProfitBuildingSpecialist

Listen to several Podcast appearances on a variety of topics:

https://www.listennotes.com/search/?q=amy%20rose%20herrick&sort_by_date=0&scope=episode&offset=0&language=Any%20language&len_min=0

Read Amy's articles on Medium at :
https://medium.com/search?q=amy+rose+herrick

Reach out to Amy at Amy@AmyRoseHerrick.com to inquire about booking Amy to be on your show as a guest or for autographed copies.

Watch one of Amy's full length financial literacy building educational videos on YouTube

https://www.youtube.com/@amyprofitspecialist

Linked in: https://www.linkedin.com/in/amyroseherrick/

Instagram: amyroseherrick

Alignable: https://www.alignable.com/christiansted-vi/amy-rose-herrick-chfc-americas-profit-building-specialist

Amazon all current titles for sale link:

https://www.amazon.com/s?k=amy+rose+herrick&crid=SGL1PH GTWZS5&sprefix=amy+rose+herrick%2Caps%2C179&ref=nb_sb _noss_1

Other titles available now, or coming soon, in the **MONEY WITH AMY SERIES** that may be of interest to you:

MONEY WITH AMY SERIES

HOW TO IDENTIFY
A QUALIFIED
ADVISOR

Exclusive Reader Gift - Details Inside

Amy Rose Herrick
Profit-Building Specialist
International Best Selling Author

Free Audio Version Included

MONEY WITH AMY SERIES

Protecting Your Health and
Wealth:
Your Step-by-Step Guide for
Multi-Generational Medical
Planning

Exclusive Reader
Gift - Details Inside

Amy Rose Herrick
Profit-Building Specialist
International Best Selling Author

Free Audio Version Included

MONEY WITH AMY SERIES

Building your
foundation:
ENTREPRENEURIAL
MISTAKES TO AVOID

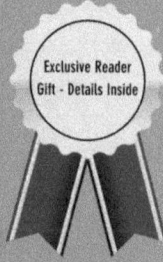

Exclusive Reader
Gift - Details Inside

Amy Rose Herrick

Profit-Building Specialist
International Best Selling Author

Free Audio Version Included

MONEY WITH AMY SERIES

REMARRIAGE:
25 QUESTIONS TO ASK
AND ANSWER
BEFORE REMARRIAGE

Exclusive Reader
Gift - Details Inside

Amy Rose Herrick

Profit-Building Specialist
International Best Selling Author

Free Audio Version Included

MONEY WITH AMY SERIES

MARRIAGE AFTER RETIREMENT:

Exclusive Reader Gift - Details Inside

25 QUESTIONS TO ASK AND ANSWER BEFORE YOU MARRY

Amy Rose Herrick

Profit-Building Specialist
International Best Selling Author

🎧 Free Audio Version Included

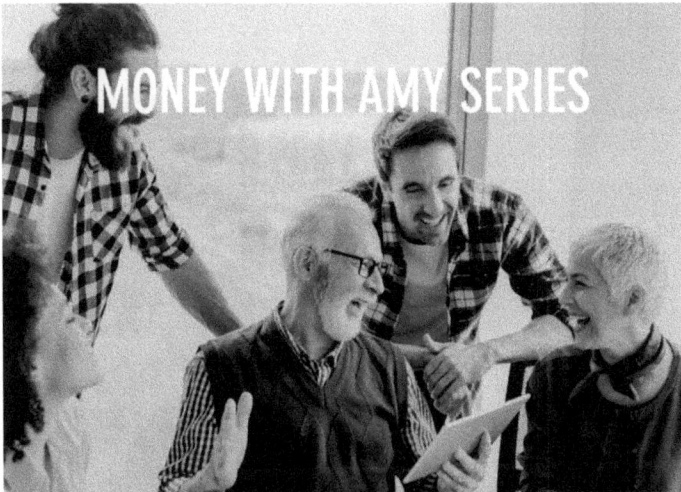

MONEY WITH AMY SERIES

Self-Employed Taxes:

Unleashing Schedule C
Deductions A Line-By-Line
Guide to Unlock Deductions
and Create New Tax Savings
for Small Business Owners
and Independent Contractors

Exclusive Reader
Gift - Details Inside

Amy Rose Herrick

Profit-Building Specialist
International Best Selling Author

Free Audio Version Included

MONEY WITH AMY SERIES

The Profitable
Entrepreneur:
16 Ways to Retrain Entrepreneurs
Using Mindset, Time
Management, Leveraging Your
Resources and Enjoying More
Business Travel Inexpensively

Exclusive Reader
Gift - Details Inside

Amy Rose Herrick

Profit-Building Specialist
International Best Selling Author

Free Audio Version Included

www.ingramcontent.com/pod-product-compliance
Lightning Source LLC
Chambersburg PA
CBHW060252030426
42335CB00014B/1658